Word Study in Action

Words Their Way

Word Study Notebook

Donald R. Bear • Marcia Invernizzi • Francine Johnston

Contents

continued next page

CELEBRATION PRESS
Pearson Learning Group

The following people have contributed to the development of this product:

Art and Design: Dorothea Fox, Jane Heelan

Editorial: Leslie Feierstone-Barna, Linda Dorf, Linette Mathewson, Tracey Randinelli

Inventory: Yvette Higgins

Marketing: Christine Fleming

Production/Manufacturing: Alan Dalgleish

Publishing Operations: Jennifer Van Der Heide

COVER ART: Andrew Lessel, age 8; Katia Walters, age 8; Natasha Walters, age 10.

Celebration Press® is a registered trademark of Addison-Wesley Educational Publishers, Inc. Words Their Way™ is a trademark of Pearson Education, Inc.

ISBN 0-7652-6761-6

Printed in the United States of America
8 9 10   08 07

Celebration Press

Pearson Learning Group

1-800-321-3106
www.pearsonlearning.com

Long Vowel Patterns CVCe

make	huge	stove	drive
hose	mice	face	June
hike	cube	joke	same
rude	gate	life	rode
base	hole	flute	nine
rope	prize	page	use

Long Vowel Patterns CVCe

ā	ī	ō	ū
rake	five	globe	mule

Sort 1: Long Vowel Patterns CVCe　(5)

Say each long vowel word. Write on the lines words from the box that show each long vowel sound.

drive	stove	huge	make	June	face	mice	hose
same	joke	cube	hike	rode	life	gate	rude
nine	flute	hole	base	use	page	prize	rope

ā	ī	ō	ū
rake	five	globe	mule

Long Vowel Patterns CVVC ai, oa, ee, ea, ui, oo

float	speak	train	broom	suit
bruise	tail	coat	heat	sleep
soap	green	team	juice	spoon
pain	mood	toast	teeth	peach
	smooth	cruise	chain	week

Sort 2: Long Vowel Patterns CVVC ai, oa, ee, ea, ui, oo

āi	ōa	ēe
rain	road	feet

ēa	ūi	ōo
mean	fruit	food

Draw a picture of something whose name contains the long vowel sound and spelling pattern shown. Write the name below each picture.

āi	ōa	ēe
rain	road	feet

ēa	ūi	ōo
mean	fruit	food

Long Vowel Patterns VCC-igh and Open Syllables
-y, -ay, -ew, and -ow

high	flow	tray	know	fly
grow	sky	bright	flew	clay
stay	stew	throw	shy	sigh
cry	sight	blew	hay	slow
chew	play	try	fight	dew

Sort 3: Long Vowel Patterns VCC-igh and Open Syllables-y, -ay, -ew, and -ow (11)

Long Vowel Patterns VCC-igh and Open Syllables -y, -ay, -ew, and -ow

īgh VCC	y = ī CV	āy CVV	ēw CVV	ōw CVV
might	why	lay	new	show

Say each long vowel word. Write on the lines words from the box that show each long vowel sound.

chew	cry	stay	grow	high
play	sight	stew	sky	flow
try	blew	throw	bright	tray
fight	hay	shy	flew	know
dew	slow	sigh	clay	fly

īgh VCC	y = ī CV	āy CVV	ēw CVV	ōw CVV
might	why	lay	new	show

r-Influenced Vowel Patterns ar, ir, or, ur

start	burn	first	fork
horn	harm	hurt	dirt
curl	birth	north	sharp
corn	dark	swirl	burst
stir	surf	storm	harp
porch	girl	curb	shark

Sort 4: r-Influenced Vowel Patterns ar, ir, or, ur

r-Influenced Vowel Patterns are, ire, ore, ure, air, ear

dear	pare	fair	tore
more	stair	lure	wire
pure	fare	fear	bare
pair	store	tire	near
hire	year	chair	cure
		stare	wore

are	ire	ore
care	fire	shore

ure	air	ear
sure	hair	clear

Say each word aloud. Write on the lines words from the box that show each r-influenced vowel pattern.

tore	fair	pare	dear	wire	lure	stair	more
bare	fear	fare	pure	near	tire	store	pair
cure	chair	year	hire	wore	stare		

care	fire	shore
_____	_____	_____
_____	_____	_____
_____	_____	_____
_____	_____	_____
_____	_____	_____

sure	hair	clear
_____	_____	_____
_____	_____	_____
_____	_____	_____
_____	_____	_____

Sort 5: r-Influenced Vowel Patterns are, ire, ore, ure, air, ear

soy	join	clown
cloud	found	growl
joy	soil	owl
ground	spoil	toy
crown	pound	ploy
coil	shout	moist
drown	decoy	enjoy
frown	count	coin

Diphthongs oi, oy, ou, ow

oi	oy	ou	ow
point	boy	sound	brown

sp	j	p	cl	sh	n	l	c	t	d	gr	cr

oi	oy	ou	ow

almost	paw	cause
bought	fought	fault
straw	also	yawn
brought	pause	tall
taught	shawl	calm
ought	stalk	vault
cough	hawk	haunt
law	chalk	trough

ou						
thought						

al						
small						

au						
caught						

aw						
saw						

Sort 7: Ambiguous Vowels aw, au, al, ou

(29)

Choose beginning and ending letters to make words with *aw, au, al,* or *ou.* Write each word on a line.

str	sh	se	ch	st	b	c	l	nt	t	k	gh

aw	au	al	ou

tied	missed
hair	tail
sale	maid
hymn	hare
by	right
ring	mist
knight	him
bye	sail
made	eight
write	tide
ate	wring
night	tale

find	fined

Say each word aloud. Write on the line a word that sounds the same but is spelled differently and has a different meaning. Then write a sentence that uses the new word.

tied _____

missed _____

hare _____

tail _____

sale _____

maid _____

bye _____

write _____

knight _____

ate _____

hymn _____

ring _____

scrape	strange	spray
throw	shrink	squish
scratch	spruce	strict
throne	shrunk	squash
through	spread	string
scrap	shriek	squeeze
sprain	threat	stream
scream	shrimp	squeak

scr	str	spr
screen	strong	spring

thr	shr	squ
three	shred	square

Write on the lines words that begin with scr, str, spr, thr, shr, or squ.

scr	str	spr
_____	_____	_____
_____	_____	_____
_____	_____	_____
_____	_____	_____
_____	_____	_____

thr	shr	squ
_____	_____	_____
_____	_____	_____
_____	_____	_____
_____	_____	_____

Sort 9: Three-Letter Blends scr, str, spr, thr, shr, squ

tease	prince	leave
dance	choose	twelve
glove	fence	cheese
piece	loose	solve
wise	prove	peace
shove	sense	bounce

-ce	-ve	-se
chance	move	please

Choose beginning and middle letters to make words with ending letters
-ce, -ve, and -se. Write each word on a line.

| ch | pr | p | b | gl | l | s | t | pl | o | an | in | en | ea | oo | ee | ie |

-ce	-ve	-se

badge	charge	stage
rage	ridge	surge
range	judge	cage
huge	fudge	change
dodge	page	sponge
bridge	bulge	

-dge	-ge	r, l, n + -ge
edge	age	large

Write on the lines words that end in -dge or -ge.

-dge	-ge

witch	torch	roach
screech	gulch	pitch
coach	bench	sketch
which	fetch	branch
beach	rich	match
speech	much	crunch
hutch	teach	French

-tch	-ch	r, l, n + -ch	Oddball
catch	reach	porch	

Sort 12: Word Endings -tch, -ch

Write on the lines words that end with -tch or -ch.

-tch	-ch

Sort 12: Word Endings -tch, -ch

couldn't	they'll
that'll	wouldn't
aren't	weren't
this'll	who'll
she'll	isn't
shouldn't	doesn't
you'll	he'll

not	will

Read each contraction. Write the two words that make up each contraction. Then circle the letters that are dropped when the contraction is formed.

they'll _____

wouldn't _____

that'll _____

this'll _____

aren't _____

who'll _____

weren't _____

isn't _____

she'll _____

shouldn't _____

you'll _____

he'll _____

doesn't _____

who's	could've
I've	there's
he's	here's
would've	should've
they've	she's
where's	what's
might've	you've

is	have

Read each contraction. Write the two words that make up each contraction. Then circle the letters that are dropped when the contraction is formed.

could've _____

I've _____

there's _____

he's _____

here's _____

would've _____

should've _____

she's _____

they've _____

where's _____

what's _____

might've _____

you've _____

Sort 14: Contractions is, have

rest	yell	run	swim
standing	jump	sit	passing
pick	put	yelling	swimming
putting	pass	stand	running
picking	jumping	resting	sitting

Sort 15: Adding -ing to Words With VC and VCC Patterns

+ -ing	VCC base word	double + -ing	VC base word
asking	ask	getting	get

Sort 15: Adding -ing to Words With VC and VCC Patterns

Complete each sentence by adding the ending -ing to the word in parentheses. Write the word on the line.

My neighbor is _____ flowers from his garden. (pick)

Rosa is _____ in a race this weekend. (run)

My mother and I like _____ together on the sofa. (rest)

Luke is _____ the ball to his teammate. (pass)

Jamal likes _____ on the park bench. (sit)

Kyle thinks _____ rope is fun. (jump)

The librarian is _____ away the returned books. (put)

Ling enjoys _____ each day after school. (swim)

Our teacher doesn't like _____ in the classroom. (yell)

Pablo gets bored _____ around. (stand)

The weather is _____ better. (get)

Sarah can't go without first _____ her parents. (ask)

Sort 15: Adding -ing to Words With VC and VCC Patterns

meeting	trading	moan	close
dream	write	skating	mailing
waving	closing	clean	wave
meet	trade	dreaming	moaning
cleaning	writing	mail	skate

+ -ing	VVC base word	e-drop + -ing	VCe base word
eating	eat	using	use

Sort 16: Adding -ing to Words With VCe and VVC Patterns

(65)

Make new words by adding the ending -ing to the following base words. Write the new words on the lines. Then write a sentence containing each new word.

close _____

moan _____

write _____

dream _____

wave _____

clean _____

trade _____

meet _____

skate _____

mail _____

use _____

eat _____

Sort 16: Adding -ing to Words With VCe and VVC Patterns

spelling	adding	moving	cutting
floating	humming	living	stopping
grinning	chewing	begging	coming
snowing	jogging	taking	talking
smiling	pushing	having	working

Review of Inflected Ending -ing

double + -ing	e-drop + -ing	+ -ing
setting	hiking	reading

Make new words by adding the ending -ing to the following base words. Write the new words on the lines.

cut _____

move _____

add _____

spell _____

stop _____

live _____

hum _____

float _____

come _____

beg _____

chew _____

grin _____

talk _____

take _____

jog _____

snow _____

work _____

have _____

push _____

smile _____

hike _____

read _____

Adding -ed to Words With VC, VCe, VVC, and VCC Patterns

wanted	waited	saved	mixed	planned
nodded	closed	helped	grabbed	seemed
shouted	hunted	stepped	liked	started
named	called	lived	dropped	passed

Sort 18: Adding -ed to Words With VC, VCe, VVC, and VCC Patterns

Adding -ed to Words With VC, VCe, VVC, and VCC Patterns

VC	VCe	VVC	VCC	Oddball
hopped	hoped	joined	acted	

Sort 18: Adding -ed to Words With VC, VCe, VVC, and VCC Patterns   (73)

Make new words by adding the ending -ed to the following base words. Write the new words on the lines.

plan	_____	step	_____
mix	_____	hunt	_____
save	_____	shout	_____
wait	_____	pass	_____
want	_____	drop	_____
seem	_____	live	_____
grab	_____	call	_____
help	_____	name	_____
close	_____	hop	_____
nod	_____	hope	_____
start	_____	join	_____
like	_____	act	_____

Sort 18: Adding -ed to Words With VC, VCe, VVC, and VCC Patterns

keep	shone
threw	freeze
slide	kept
froze	drive
bleed	slid
drew	sweep
know	drove
bled	draw
shine	knew
swept	throw

present	past
sleep	slept

Write the irregular past-tense form of each verb on the line. Then write a sentence containing the past-tense verb.

sleep _____

keep _____

draw _____

shine _____

sweep _____

throw _____

know _____

freeze _____

drive _____

slide _____

bleed _____

watches	sketches	scratches	brushes
eyelashes	ashes	splashes	guesses
foxes	speeches	mixes	places
crashes	peaches	voices	branches
leashes	changes	horses	kisses

add -s	add -es -s	add -es -x	add -es -sh	add -es -ch

Make each of the following singular words plural by adding -s or -es. Write the words on the lines.

singular	plural	singular	plural
brush	_____	place	_____
kiss	_____	splash	_____
voice	_____	sketch	_____
speech	_____	change	_____
eyelash	_____	crash	_____
guess	_____	branch	_____
scratch	_____	mix	_____
horse	_____	ash	_____
peach	_____	watch	_____
fox	_____	leash	_____

Unusual Plurals

goose	knife	life	leaf
knives	mouse	women	deer
mice	geese	teeth	wolves
leaves	tooth	woman	loaf
wolf	sheep	loaves	lives

Unusual Plurals

-f or -fe to -ves		vowel change		no change
wife	wives	foot	feet	

Underline the word in each sentence that means more than one. Then write the singular form of the word on the line.

Devon thinks his cat will have nine lives. _____

Look at the geese flying through the air. _____

The kitchen knives are kept on the counter. _____

Ella often sees deer in her backyard. _____

Mia makes loaves of bread each week. _____

There were mice on the farm. _____

At night I hear wolves howling. _____

There are many women at the store. _____

Raj pet the sheep at the zoo. _____

My mother brushes her teeth after she eats. _____

The restaurant had a party for the wives. _____

Lily dipped her feet in the pool. _____

Sort 21: Unusual Plurals

Word Endings -y, -ey, -ie

money	rely	sky
fifty	honey	cookie
angry	try	ready
every	jockey	goalie
chimney	plenty	body
pinkie	hockey	empty

Word Endings -y, -ey, -ie

-y = ī	-ie = ē	-ey = ē	-y = ē
July	movie	turkey	many

Sort 22: Word Endings -y, -ey, -ie

(89)

-y = ē	-ey = ē	-ie = ē	-y = ī
many	turkey	movie	July

Sort 22: Word Endings -y, -ey, -ie

monkeys	babies	ponies
stories	alleys	parties
valleys	trays	ladies
fireflies	boys	toys
donkeys	candies	duties
berries	journeys	families

Plural Endings: Final -y

-y to i + -es					
cities					

+ -s					
plays					

Make each of the following singular words plural. Write the plural words on the lines.

singular	plural	singular	plural
monkey	_____	boy	_____
baby	_____	toy	_____
pony	_____	donkey	_____
story	_____	candy	_____
alley	_____	duty	_____
party	_____	berry	_____
valley	_____	journey	_____
tray	_____	family	_____
lady	_____	play	_____
firefly	_____	city	_____

Sort 23: Plural Endings: Final -y

replied	copying	enjoys
hurrying	stayed	studies
carries	copied	replying
studied	staying	enjoyed
carrying	hurried	replies
copies	enjoying	carried
hurries	stays	studying

+ -ing	+ -s or -y to i + -es	+ -ed or -y to i + -ed
crying	cries	cried

Read each word. Make new words by adding the endings -ing, -s or -es, and -ed. (Change y to i as necessary.) Write the new words in the correct columns.

	-ing	-s or + -es	-ed
reply			
copy			
enjoy			
hurry			
stay			
study			
carry			
cry			

Sort 24: Adding Inflected Endings -s, -ed, and -ing to Words With Final -y

Compound Words

bookmark	snowflake	downstairs	headfirst	lightweight
headlight	daylight	snowstorm	bookworm	downtown
cookbook	downpour	headphones	flashlight	snowplow
countdown	scrapbook	snowball	headstrong	sunlight

Compound Words

snowman				

headache				

downhill				

lighthouse				

bookcase				

Choose words from the box to make new words. Write the words and the compound words on the lines. Draw a picture to illustrate each compound word.

light	house	sun	book	snow
worm	cook	head	phones	man

_____ + _____ = _____

_____ + _____ = _____

_____ + _____ = _____

_____ + _____ = _____

_____ + _____ = _____

_____ + _____ = _____

More Compound Words

nothing	sometime	outfit	somehow	anything
herself	myself	somewhere	themselves	beside
sideways	itself	outside	yourself	someone
	something	throughout	outfield	checkout

inside	without	everything	himself	somebody

Choose words from the box to make new words. On the lines, write the two words that make up the compound word, and the compound word itself. You may use each word more than once.

any	them	selves	some	thing
her	check	in	my	self

be	your	through	no	one	out	side	time
ways	how	where	it	body	him	every	with

dinner	pretty	diner
tiger	penny	later
paper	puppy	rabbit
even	over	kitten
hello	ruler	lesson
busy	crazy	summer
open	happy	tiny

Syllable Juncture in VCV and VCCV Patterns

-VCV-	-VCCV-	Oddball
super	supper	

Sort 27: Syllable Juncture in VCV and VCCV Patterns

Read each of the words in the box. Write the words in
the correct column. Break the words into two syllables
by drawing a line between the two syllables.

dinner	pretty	diner	tiger	penny	later
paper	rabbit	even	over	kitten	hello
lesson	busy	crazy	summer	open	happy

-VCV-	-VCCV-	Oddball
su/per	sup/per	
_____	_____	_____
_____	_____	_____
_____	_____	_____
_____	_____	_____
_____	_____	_____
_____	_____	_____
_____	_____	_____
_____	_____	_____
_____	_____	_____

Sort 27: Syllable Juncture in VCV and VCCV Patterns

follow	female	matter	winter
number	final	water	problem
yellow	fever	finger	butter
bottom	member	pattern	sister
blanket	pillow	moment	chapter

More Syllable Junctures in VCV and VCCV Patterns

-VCV-	-VCCV- doublet	-VCCV- different	Oddball
silent	happen	basket	

Sort 28: More Syllable Junctures in VCV and VCCV Patterns

Read each of the words in the box. Write the words in the correct column. Break the words into two syllables by drawing a line between the two syllables.

winter	matter	female	follow	problem	water	final	number
butter	finger	fever	yellow	sister	pattern	member	moment

-VCV- si/lent	-VCCV- doublet hap/pen	-VCCV- different bas/ket	Oddball

Syllable Juncture in VCV and VVCV Patterns

never	pilot	trainer	river
student	peanut	planet	frozen
seven	humor	finish	leader
second	sneaker	present	lazy
lemon	music	minute	easy

Syllable Juncture in VCV and VVCV Patterns

-V/CV- long	-VC/V- short	-VVCV- long
human	wagon	reason

Read each of the words in the box. Write the words in the correct column. Break the words into two syllables by drawing a line between the two syllables.

river	seven	never	sneaker	peanut	minute	finish
humor	pilot	present	planet	easy	leader	lemon
trainer	lazy	frozen	second	student	music	

-V/CV- long	-VC/V- short	-VVCV- long
hu/man	wag/on	rea/son
_____	_____	_____
_____	_____	_____
_____	_____	_____
_____	_____	_____
_____	_____	_____
_____	_____	_____
_____	_____	_____
_____	_____	_____

Syllable Juncture in VCCCV and VV Patterns

riot	kingdom	complete	poet
halfway	monster	area	pumpkin
cruel	English	trial	kitchen
hundred	lion	control	mushroom
children	video	inspect	diet

Sort 30: Syllable Juncture in VCCCV and VV Patterns (119)

-VCC/CV-	-VC/CCV-	-VV-
athlete	pilgrim	create

Read each of the words in the box. Write the words in the correct column. Break the words into two syllables by drawing a line between the two syllables.

poet	complete	riot	kingdom	pumpkin	halfway	monster
area	kitchen	trial	English	cruel	mushroom	control
lion	hundred	diet	inspect	video	children	

-VCC/CV-	-VC/CCV-	-VV-
ath/lete	pil/grim	cre/ate

plotting	meeting	quoted
waited	faded	spelling
writing	nodded	shouting
acted	floated	skated
wanted	saving	standing
needed	hunted	taking
getting	using	leaking

-VCV-	-VCCV-	-VVCV-
hoping	hopping	cleaning

Read each of the words in the box. Write the words in the correct column. Break the words into two syllables by drawing a line between the two syllables.

plotting	meeting	quoted	waited	faded	spelling	writing
nodded	shouting	acted	floated	skated	wanted	saving
standing	needed	hunted	taking	getting	using	leaking

-VCV-	-VCCV-	-VVCV-
hop/ing	hop/ping	clean/ing

complain	painter	decay
mistake	crayon	parade
chocolate	mayor	maybe
escape	bracelet	amaze
pavement	basement	explain
railroad	raisin	today
remain	payment	obey

Long a Patterns in Accented Syllables

ā in 1st Syllable	ā in 2nd Syllable	Oddball
rainbow	awake	

Read each of the long a words in the box. Write the words in the column that shows the vowel pattern they contain. Draw a line between the two syllables. Then underline the accented syllable.

complain	painter	decay	mistake	crayon
parade	railroad	mayor	maybe	escape
bracelet	amaze	pavement	basement	explain

āi	ā_e	āy
rain/bow	a/wake	pay/ment
_____	_____	_____
_____	_____	_____
_____	_____	_____
_____	_____	_____
_____	_____	_____
_____	_____	_____
_____	_____	_____

delight	ninety	surprise
machine	decide	higher
advice	brightly	survive
forgive	driveway	combine
slightly	arrive	lightning
provide	sidewalk	favorite
invite	highway	describe

Long i Patterns in Accented Syllables

Oddball					

ī in 2ⁿᵈ syllable					
polite					

ī in 1ˢᵗ syllable					
frighten					

Sort 33: Long i Patterns in Accented Syllables (133)

Read each of the long i words in the box. Write the words in the column that shows the vowel pattern they contain. Draw a line between the two syllables. Then underline the accented syllable.

delight	ninety	surprise	machine	decide	higher	advice
brightly	survive	forgive	driveway	combine	slightly	arrive
lightning	provide	sidewalk	favorite	invite	highway	describe

īgh	ī_e	Oddball
fright/en	po/lite	
‎	‎	‎
‎	‎	‎
‎	‎	‎
‎	‎	‎
‎	‎	‎
‎	‎	‎
‎	‎	‎
‎	‎	‎
‎	‎	‎

explode	hostess	suppose
lonely	compose	owner
bureau	lower	decode
lonesome	remote	loafer
alone	closely	Europe
soapy	approach	poster
awoke	postage	erode

Long o Patterns in Accented Syllables

ō in 1st syllable		ō in 2nd syllable		Oddball
toaster		below		

Read each of the long o words in the box. Write the words in the column that shows the vowel pattern they contain. Draw a line between the two syllables. Then underline the accented syllable.

hostess	suppose	lonely	compose	owner	closely
decode	lower	remote	loafer	alone	erode
soapy	approach	poster	awoke	postage	

ōa	ō_e	ōCC or ōw
toas/ter	ex/plode	be/low
_____	_____	_____
_____	_____	_____
_____	_____	_____
_____	_____	_____
_____	_____	_____
_____	_____	_____
_____	_____	_____
_____	_____	_____

amuse	Tuesday	perfume
useful	pollute	moody
confuse	doodle	reduce
toothache	balloon	scooter
shampoo	beauty	cartoon
cougar	conclude	noodle

Long u Patterns in Accented Syllables

ū in 2ⁿᵈ syllable

include

ū in 1ˢᵗ syllable

rooster

Sort 35: Long u Patterns in Accented Syllables

Read each of the long u words in the box. Write the words in the column that shows the vowel pattern they contain. Draw a line between the two syllables. Then underline the accented syllable.

amuse	Tuesday	perfume	useful	pollute	moody
confuse	doodle	reduce	toothache	balloon	scooter
shampoo	beauty	cartoon	cougar	conclude	noodle

o͞o	u̅_e	Oddball
roos/ter	in/clude	

leather	increase	season
compete	reader	heavy
defeat	pleasant	feature
sweater	freedom	indeed
meaning	steady	extreme
fifteen	eastern	repeat
people	healthy	thirteen

ē in 1ˢᵗ syllable	ĕ in 1ˢᵗ syllable	ē in 2ⁿᵈ syllable
needle	feather	succeed

Read each of the words in the box. Write the words in the column that shows the vowel pattern and sound they contain. Draw a line between the two syllables. Then underline the accented syllable.

leather	increase	sweater	compete	reader	heavy	defeat
pleasant	feature	freedom	indeed	meaning	steady	thirteen
extreme	fifteen	eastern	repeat	healthy		

ēe or ē_e	ĕa	ēa
nee/dle	feath/er	sea/son

Sort 36: Short and Long e Patterns in Accented Syllables

Listen to each word as it is read aloud. Write the word in the box that shows its correct vowel pattern.

CVCe	CVVC	CV

CVV	VCC

Listen to each word as it is read aloud. Write the word in the box that shows its correct r-influenced vowel pattern.

ar	ir	or	ur

Spell Check 1b: Short r-Influenced Vowel Patterns

Listen to each word as it is read aloud. Write the word in the box that shows its correct r-influenced vowel pattern.

are	ire	ore

ure	air	ear

oi coil		oy soy

ou ground		ow crown

aw paw	au vault	al stalk

ou fought

SPELL CHECK 2a

Read each word in the column on the left. Then write a homophone for the word in the column on the right.

1. tide	1. _____
2. missed	2. _____
3. hair	3. _____
4. tail	4. _____
5. sale	5. _____
6. made	6. _____
7. by	7. _____
8. eye	8. _____
9. night	9. _____
10. eight	10. _____

Spell Check 2b: Homophones   251

Listen to each word as it is read aloud. Write the word in the box that shows its correct beginning blend.

scr	str	spr
_____	_____	_____
_____	_____	_____
_____	_____	_____
_____	_____	_____

thr	shr	squ
_____	_____	_____
_____	_____	_____
_____	_____	_____
_____	_____	_____

SPELL CHECK 3b

Listen to each word as it is read aloud. Write the word in the box that shows its correct word ending.

-dge	-ve	-ce	-se

-ch	-tch	-ge

Listen to each word as it is read aloud. Write the word in the box that shows the correct type of contraction.

not	will	is	have

Read each base word. Then add each word ending to the base word and write the new word in the correct column.

Base Word	Add -s or -es	Add -ed	Add -ing
1. trip	1.	1.	1.
2. chase	2.	2.	2.
3. need	3.	3.	3.
4. dress	4.	4.	4.
5. dry	5.	5.	5.
6. tax	6.	6.	6.
7. fan	7.	7.	7.
8. race	8.	8.	8.
9. play	9.	9.	9.

Listen to each word as it is read aloud. Write the word in the box that shows the correct type of compound word.

snow _____

_____ side

side _____

_____ self

self book _____

_____ light

light _____

_____ book

SPELL CHECK 6

Listen to each word as it is read aloud. Write the word in the box that shows its correct syllable juncture.

SPELL CHECK 7

-VCCV-	-VCCCV-	-VC/V- short

-V/CV- long	-VVCV-	-VV-

Listen to each word as it is read aloud. Write the words on the lines.

1. _____

2. _____

3. _____

4. _____

5. _____

6. _____

7. _____

8. _____

9. _____

10. _____

11. _____

12. _____

13. _____

14. _____

15. _____

16. _____

17. _____

18. _____

19. _____

20. _____

21. _____

22. _____